Disney SONGS FOR TWO

Disney Characters and Artwork
TM & © 2018 Disney

*TARZAN® Owned by Edgar Rice Burroughs, Inc.
And Used by Permission
© Burroughs/Disney

The following songs are the property of:

Bourne Co.
Music Publishers
5 West 37th Street
New York, NY 10018

HEIGH-HO
SOME DAY MY PRINCE WILL COME
WHEN YOU WISH UPON A STAR
WHISTLE WHILE YOU WORK
WHO'S AFRAID OF THE BIG BAD WOLF?

Arrangements by Mark Phillips

ISBN 978-1-5400-3710-7

Visit Hal Leonard Online at
www.halleonard.com

Contact Us:
Hal Leonard
7777 West Bluemound Road
Milwaukee, WI 53213
Email: info@halleonard.com

In Europe contact:
Hal Leonard Europe Limited
42 Wigmore Street
Marylebone, London, W1U 2RN
Email: info@halleonardeurope.com

In Australia contact:
Hal Leonard Australia Pty. Ltd.
4 Lentara Court
Cheltenham, Victoria, 3192 Australia
Email: info@halleonard.com.au

BEAUTY AND THE BEAST

from BEAUTY AND THE BEAST

ALTO SAXES

Music by ALAN MENKEN
Lyrics by HOWARD ASHMAN

3

BIBBIDI-BOBBIDI-BOO

(The Magic Song)

from CINDERELLA

ALTO SAXES

Words by JERRY LIVINGSTON
Music by MACK DAVID
and AL HOFFMAN

Brightly, in 2

CAN YOU FEEL THE LOVE TONIGHT

from THE LION KING

ALTO SAXES

Music by ELTON JOHN
Lyrics by TIM RICE

CHIM CHIM CHER-EE

from MARY POPPINS

ALTO SAXES

Words and Music by RICHARD M. SHERMAN
and ROBERT B. SHERMAN

CIRCLE OF LIFE

from THE LION KING

ALTO SAXES

Music by ELTON JOHN
Lyrics by TIM RICE

COLORS OF THE WIND

from POCAHONTAS

ALTO SAXES

Music by ALAN MENKEN
Lyrics by STEPHEN SCHWARTZ

EVERMORE
from BEAUTY AND THE BEAST

ALTO SAXES

Music by ALAN MENKEN
Lyrics by TIM RICE

FRIEND LIKE ME

from ALADDIN

ALTO SAXES

Music by ALAN MENKEN
Lyrics by HOWARD ASHMAN

17

HEIGH-HO
The Dwarfs' Marching Song from SNOW WHITE AND THE SEVEN DWARFS

ALTO SAXES

Words by LARRY MOREY
Music by FRANK CHURCHILL

Moderately, in 2

HOW FAR I'LL GO
from MOANA

ALTO SAXES

Music and Lyrics by
LIN-MANUEL MIRANDA

LET IT GO

from FROZEN

ALTO SAXES

Music and Lyrics by KRISTEN ANDERSON-LOPEZ
and ROBERT LOPEZ

MICKEY MOUSE MARCH

from THE MICKEY MOUSE CLUB

ALTO SAXES

Words and Music by
JIMMIE DODD

SOME DAY MY PRINCE WILL COME
from SNOW WHITE AND THE SEVEN DWARFS

ALTO SAXES

Words by LARRY MOREY
Music by FRANK CHURCHILL

SOMETHING THERE

from BEAUTY AND THE BEAST

ALTO SAXES

Music by ALAN MENKEN
Lyrics by HOWARD ASHMAN

Moderately fast

SUPERCALIFRAGILISTICEXPIALIDOCIOUS

from MARY POPPINS

ALTO SAXES

Words and Music by RICHARD M. SHERMAN
and ROBERT B. SHERMAN

D.C. al Fine

WHEN SHE LOVED ME

from TOY STORY 2

ALTO SAXES

Music and Lyrics by
RANDY NEWMAN

WHEN YOU WISH UPON A STAR

from PINOCCHIO

ALTO SAXES

Words by NED WASHINGTON
Music by LEIGH HARLINE

WHISTLE WHILE YOU WORK

from SNOW WHITE AND THE SEVEN DWARFS

ALTO SAXES

Words by LARRY MOREY
Music by FRANK CHURCHILL

Moderately, in 2

WHO'S AFRAID OF THE BIG BAD WOLF?

from THREE LITTLE PIGS

ALTO SAXES

Words and Music by
FRANK CHURCHILL
Additional Lyric by ANN RONELL

A WHOLE NEW WORLD

from ALADDIN

ALTO SAXES

Music by ALAN MENKEN
Lyrics by TIM RICE

YOU'LL BE IN MY HEART
(Pop Version)
from TARZAN®

ALTO SAXES

Words and Music by
PHIL COLLINS

YOU'RE WELCOME

from MOANA

ALTO SAXES

Music and Lyrics by
LIN-MANUEL MIRANDA

ZIP-A-DEE-DOO-DAH

from SONG OF THE SOUTH

ALTO SAXES

Words by RAY GILBERT
Music by ALLIE WRUBEL

Brightly, in 2